THE
Girl
IN THE MIRROR

Shauntasha Toombs

Book Cover Design: Prize Publishing House

Printed by: Prize Publishing House, LLC in the United States of America.

First printing edition 2023.

Prize Publishing House
P.O. Box 9856, Chesapeake, VA 23321
www.PrizePublishingHouse.com

Library of Congress Control Number: 2023907476

ISBN (Paperback): 979-8-9875046-4-2
ISBN (E-Book): 979-8-9875046-5-9

CONTENTS

This book is dedicated to the people who have faced many obstacles in life, not knowing if they'll ever overcome them. I'm here to tell you that if God did it for me, He can do it for you

You ever wondered what, or even who is
holding you back from progression?

Maybe it was a situation that left you broken, a
circumstance you couldn't overcome, a loss you never
got over, or the guilt that left you walking in shame.

That's about to change. You're about to
become the best version of yourself.

The Girl in the Mirror is a book about transformation.
In some of the worst moments of my life, she led me
to a turning point where God was getting through to
me to receive His glory. She didn't let her pain dictate
her future. Instead, she leans on God's strength and
follows the path he laid out for her to rise above it all.

Start seeing yourself how God sees you. Embrace
change and know that you are victorious.

The Girl in the Mirror

FOREWORD

Life experiences can greatly impact how you perceive oneself, others, and the external world. As humans we may suppress painful emotions to avoid addressing problems or sweep them under the rug, for a better lack of words. If problems are not worked through, it's unlikely you will move on from the past. You will transfer negative feelings from the past onto others in the present. Nicole courageously shares traumatic life experiences that impacted her mental well-being. She revisits critical periods of her life from childhood to adulthood that she worked through on her healing journey to improve her mental health and live her self-truth. Through her healing journey, she developed self-awareness in therapy. She shares with you her dysfunctional familial patterns and life challenges that some are afraid of sharing. It was through an act of courage, resilience, and vulnerability she frees herself from thoughts, experiences, and fears. This book should be used as a tool to encourage you to live your truth and to instill hope, support, and compassion in others that may have similar life experiences. Nicole wants you to know you are not alone.

"Don't quit; nurture your growth, and strive to be a healthier you." - Crystal Mullen-Johnson

Crystal Mullen-Johnson, LICSW-PIP, RPT

Licensed Clinical Social Worker

Strive Counseling Services, CEO/Founder

INTRODUCTION

Living in total freedom is something I never imagined would bring me so much peace and joy. God had been tugging on me night after night until I finally said, "Yes, Lord, whatever it takes to get some rest"; at least, that's what I thought would happen. The rest didn't come right then, but the thoughts and actions that had me in bondage were brought to light. Even though I wanted deliverance and growth, I didn't want the discomfort that came with it. I just wanted things to go back to normal. But to go back would mean *my* broken way of thinking. And you know what they say, "You are what you think." So, I had to tighten up my shoelaces and prepare for the race. Every second that passes you by is transforming you, whether you know it or not.

As I wrote this book, my entire life changed with every stroke against the keyboard. It's triggering to relive some of these memories I am writing about. The same memories that kept me in bondage. But it was also necessary to do the work of finding my true, authentic self.

I remember telling myself that if I could just get over this one thing, I'd be fine. Still, one thing came after another, affecting me internally, and it was never-ending. My journey taught me about myself and what perseverance meant for my life. I have pushed myself so much that I now know no matter how intense the resistance is, you must be willing to push through it. If you are like me, sometimes you want someone in your corner to cheer you on, but what do you do when you only have yourself and your back is against the wall? Do you give up? Or do you muster up enough strength to fight on?

I've always had the tenacity to give it everything I had, but I often wondered if I was ever good enough to reach my goals. There was a reoccurring shame that came over me each time I felt defeated. There was anger that was built up. My scars constantly remind me of the levels of pain I had to bear. Those scars from the ones you loved caused you to live in fear. Fear forced me to stay guarded and not let anyone in, but who was I really keeping out? Myself?

But just like that, God wasn't done with me. Sometimes

it takes you losing to win. You see, in the Bible, Joseph's brothers sold him into slavery, Daniel was thrown in the lion's Den, and Job's health, wealth, and children were taken away. God had a plan for their lives, and he has one for us as well.

Even if the thoughts of doubt and fear arise as you continue to read this book, face them head-on. You can't heal what you don't confront, and this is the start of *your* journey. Look for those places in your life that were only supposed to be temporary moments where you've made a rest stop. God will turn your pain into purpose, but you must be willing to do the work; don't get sidetracked. There will be battles you have to fight, and you will get knocked down, but you don't have to stay down. Wake up each morning with the intention that you will win the day.

What are you willing to sacrifice to be used by God? He wants to use you not for your selfish ambitions but for his greater good. It's never too late, and you can start right now and at this very moment. Step out of your comfort zone and go all in. Choose to grow. Choose to believe in yourself.

His grace is sufficient.

CHAPTER 1

Childhood

As the youngest of three growing up in Asbury Park, the south side of Phenix City, Al, you'd think life would be sweet butterflies. At least, that's what I thought. Imagine growing up the only girl with no one to play with or talk to because everyone had their own agenda. My brothers could be found on the videogame, outside, riding go-karts, or playing with friends. Barbie dolls didn't excite me much, and ballet just didn't fit my personality. Each time my mom tried to force me into a dress, it was a constant battle. You know, the dresses that are poofy underneath and have an itchy slip attached to them? Yeah, that one. Until one day, I decided to hide them under my bed and lie about it. She went into my dad's closet, pulled out his thick leather belt, and tore my butt up.

It was at that moment I knew life would be a little challenging. I was entering elementary school, kindergarten, to be exact. Five houses down, Ridgecrest Elementary School sat on the top of the hill. The morning of my first day, my mother gave my brother Chris one task; to walk me home from school. Guess what. 3:00 pm had rolled around, and Chris was nowhere to be found. Tears started to stream down my face, and with a quivering voice, I asked, " Where is my brother?" I was scared, to say the least, as I began to walk down the hill and head home alone. Once I arrived, my mom greeted me at the door with a loud voice. Nicole, "Where is your brother?" looking around, I mumbled, "I don't know." Minutes later, Chris came storming into the house, asking, "Ma, where Cole at? I been looking all around that school for her?"

"Where was I?"

"Waiting in front of the school, just like I was supposed to," I responded. With a few minutes left to spare, we grabbed a snack and headed out the door to devotional training, usher board meeting, then Bible study.

With my mother being a Minister, we were in church 5 out of the 7 days of the week, and even two services on Sunday. I've always thought, "Like, who goes to church services *that* much?" Well, growing up, we did and had no other choice. Liberty Hill Missionary Baptist Church is where you'd find me most of the time. It was a nice-sized brick building with three main entrances. At that time, John F. Williams was the Pastor. His family was loving, and I looked forward to going over to their house after church on Sundays to play with their daughter. In the summertime, we looked forward to Vacation Bible School, trips to Six Flags Over Georgia, and Wild Adventures Theme Park. Growing up, our Youth Department was one of a kind. I truly appreciate my upbringing. My parents were very dedicated to us, ensuring we knew that the essence of our beings revolved around Jesus. We were brought up in the church, and my parents were blessed in their professions. My mother was a beautician, and my dad worked in the hospital. She was about 5'5 in height, brown-skinned, with long pretty hair. My dad was a darker completion and short. Everyone called him "Popeye" as a nickname. They worked long hours, day in and day out, to provide for my siblings and me. Their dedication and commitment to God, hard work, each other, and their family were my foundation for learning how to love and care for others and my sparked desire to want to impact the world.

We knew that when Friday came, we would go to our grandparents' house, making the process a norm for us. This one particular summer night, my mom had just picked us up from our grandparent's house; we were home and settled in bed. A door slammed; it was my father stumbling into the house drunk. Down the hall, he came, being loud and aggressive. He entered his bedroom and closed the door. Yelling and tossing things across the room. Fear immediately overcame me, and I instantly grabbed my pillow and buried my head to drown out the noise of his actions. I cried softly to myself because I didn't want anyone to hear me at that moment. When the noise settled, I got up and put my ear against the door to see if everything was okay; but I could only hear complete silence. The next morning, I got up to go to the restroom, opened my door, peeked across the hall into my parents' room, whose door was slightly cracked, and saw my dad lying in bed sleeping. When I entered the hallway, I could smell the residue from the alcohol (gin). It was a strong and unpleasant smell.

At the other end of the hallway, my mother was in the

kitchen cooking a large breakfast; grits, eggs, bacon, and biscuits, listening to her Gospel music. She had a plate laid out on the table for each one of us. She called for my brothers to come to the table and eat, then asked me to take my dad his plate to their room for him. I walked into the room and said, "Dad, your plate is on the dresser." He got up, still half asleep, and said," Thanks, Ma." Ma was his name for me. When I got back to the kitchen, my brothers were placed in their seats. I sat down, we said grace, and then ate. It was quiet as a mouse while we ate that morning. We never talked about what happened the night before in our household because we were always told," What goes on in this house stays in this house." So, for that incident and the future, we just went on through life, just sweeping everything under the rug.

Growing up with two brothers was very interesting, and I often wished I had a sister. I had Damion, who was the oldest. He was quiet yet sneaky. He could get away with anything. He didn't say much, but he was always there to rescue me when Chris would aggravate me. No matter what I had going on, he has always been supportive and there for me. Chris was the middle child, and our relationship had a very interesting dynamic. Let me tell you, he always wanted everything to be about him. Chris was the comedian in the family, always joking and talking about everyone who came into contact with him. Anytime he got the chance, you best believe he was bothering and pestering me. One night Chris and I were thirsty. My dad was asleep on the couch, so we tip-toed into the kitchen to get something to drink. We got the drink from the fridge, and as soon as I began to pour the juice, the cartoon surprised me by falling out of my hand, and juice went everywhere. Chris took off running down the hall, and guess who got caught? Me.

In the summertime, I looked forward to my cousin Bee coming to town from Birmingham. Me, her and my cousin, Stephanie, would stay at my great-grandmother Matilda's house on the hill. Matilda's house reminded me of *Little House on the Prairie*. Bee was my cousin on my mom's side, and we weren't too far apart in age. Bee was incredible, loud, and had that "I don't give a... *you know what*... attitude." My great grandma's house was small in size but had a lot of love within it. She had the typical air conditioner that sat in the window at your grandparent's house and that big floor heater you had to actually ignite for heat. She would grab a piece of paper, roll it up and light it, then put it against the brick. No lie, that would be the hottest heat you'd ever feel. My grandma could tell you everything that went on the hill. You want to know why? Because she would always sit up across her bed and look out the window all day long until the sun went down. We would watch *Matlock*, *In the Heat of the Night*, and *Walker Texas Ranger* in the mornings. But when one o'clock in the afternoon came, we had to be quiet or get out of the house because her stories were on.

Then there were my grandmother's neighbors. You had Shot, who stayed on the left side of my great-grandmother's house. He stayed outside in his front yard all day, waving at everyone that drove by. Then, you had Nosey D, who stayed on the other side of the house. Most times, my cousins and I would walk to Jack's, the candy store by Fred's. As we would leave my grandma's house, we had to walk up the hill, which we were always scared of doing because we might come across Miss Betsy, who was blind and in a wheelchair. She kept her door open, but no lights were ever on in there. As soon as you were going past the house, she'd roll right out onto her porch with her dogs running loose, and all we could do was look straight ahead and walk fast as hell.

Most Sundays, my mom and I would go for a drive after we got settled in from church. Our first stop would be Sonic to get some ice cream, then head on up Summerville

Road. On the North side of town, we'd go into some of the upper-echelon neighborhoods and sightsee houses. I'd always tell her that one day I'd have a home like this myself, but in reality, I imagined what life could be like if she didn't have to face some of the trials I saw her face on a daily basis. At a young age, I never understood why things were the way they were; but she assured me everything would always be all right. She stayed resilient and never let me see her sweat. My mother rarely raised her voice and always trusted that God would work everything out. She was a praying woman. Every early morning, she'd be up pleading for the blood of Jesus and calling on his name.

When Monday rolled around, my mother would call me into her room to teach me how to pay bills. She would have me count all the money first, then, from that amount, ask me how much her ten percent was so she could pay her tithes. No matter what, God was getting His first, and that's a fact. After that, she would have all her bills written down, with the amount and when they were due. After this Monday ritual, since my great-grandmother didn't drive, we'd head to her house to run errands for her. My grandmother gave exact change for all transactions, all the way down to the penny. After we paid her bills, she would have us stop and get a pack of Salem Light 100 cigarettes. We couldn't stand the smell of those things, but we never opened our mouths to tell her that out of respect.

At the time, my dad's parents lived in White Quarters by Grave Yard Street in the dead end, on the south side, off Seale Road. My Auntie Kookie stayed right beside them. There wasn't any grass in the yard, just straight dirt. Boy, did I pitch a fit when we had to go over there? All my cousins used to be there, we would be about eleven deep, with nothing to do, and my Grandma Doll would put us outside and lock the screen door early during the early morning. She fed us cold bologna sandwiches and pork n beans and weiners. If you wanted some water, you better have used the hose pipe on the side of the house because you weren't going to be "going in and out of her damn house, letting flies in." We didn't have much to do over there, but when we did get bored, we'd take the trail and go to the Candy Lady's house in the Edmond States apartments. Verbal abuse was an ordinary language in my family, with my grandparents, aunts, and uncles. It got worse when alcohol was involved. After the damage was done, they would hug and cry as if nothing had just happened. "How could this be normal?" I often thought. B**** this, and you ugly mother-you-know-what was all you heard.

In fourth grade, I met my best friend, Brittney Purnell. Inseparable we were. If you saw her, best believe I wasn't too far behind. We did just about everything together, from dressing alike, wearing our hair in those Alicia Keys braids, running summer track with Coach Fortune, AAU basketball with coach Tim, you name it, we did it. By the time we got to Junior High School, nothing had changed. We tried out for the basketball team, despite both of us being small in size. Coach Baker, her name at the time, gave me the nickname "Lil Girl." One thing about me, I was small but tough in strength. I was at the top of the key, Kitty Kat, and my best friend, BP, was on the wing; we were something serious. When I say that we had the defense on lockdown, nothing could get past us. From setting traps, rebounds, and steals, we were unstoppable. We looked forward to the game day because we'd run out at the start of the game and have the cheerleaders on each side of the team shaking their pom poms while "Bring Them Out "by T.I. was playing.

Tip-off would start, and I would be locked in and focused; nothing else mattered. As I looked into the stands, hearing the cheerleaders and crowd cheering, one thing was missing, my parents. At the time, it wasn't a big deal because I knew they had to work, but the emptiness I felt seeing other parents hug and tell their kids good job after a game, and all I had was my grandmother sitting there asking me if I was ready to go. I grabbed my bags, we left, and either she was dropping me off at the shop or to her house we went. The confusion I often felt constantly left me with unanswered questions. What was more important because I thought it was family first? Was it the streets or the church house?

CHAPTER 2

Daddy

Fathers are supposed to be a girl's first love; however, that wasn't the case for me. Don't get me wrong, I love my daddy, but watching my dad as a child and learning how a father should be as I got older, didn't reflect what I saw. My daddy is short in size and thought he was right about everything and never wrong. But not once did he show me exactly how a girl should be treated or how to change a simple tire. I didn't get the talks about boys or the father's touch. He seemed to show me everything I didn't want in a man; typical. Daddy stayed in the house, but Daddy wasn't present in my life. Traveling up the road, the backroad LP, and White Quarters is what had his attention.

My siblings and I didn't understand at the time what was transpiring because we were well taken care of and wanted for nothing. But as you get older, you realize that time is more valuable than anything.

I was an active child and tomboy at heart. I always wanted to be outside with the boys and be rough. It sucked being the only girl. My dad would fuss and never let me have a response. So, when I did talk back, and if he was in the bathroom and I walked by, he'd wet a rag twist and pop me with it or get that thick leather belt with his name engraved in it and whoop the mess out of me. What was crying? I knew I better not sniff as if the whooping hurt. This was a catalyst for how I began to hide my emotions. My oldest brother would let me in their room after I would get a whooping. I would sit on his bed, and he would comfort me. We were always taught what went on in our house and stayed in our home. Looking back now, I see that motto wasn't healthy.

Out of all the sports games I played as a child, and even through college, my dad was only present for ten. As a child, it made me feel like I wasn't good enough to be supported. Or, what was so important that he couldn't be there for me? The games and events he did show up to, he had a negative response about any little mistake I made, to the point I didn't want him there at all. Luckily, I had a good guy friend whose dad would tell me how proud he was of me and how to correct my mistakes after my games. From junior high and into my adulthood, this dad called me, checked up on me, and even talked to me about sex and boys. I cherished those moments because he instilled a lot in me.

A man is supposed to be a protector, not the one you're protected from. One day, I was home from college. My nephew, little cousin, and I were at my house. My dad came home late, drunk; my mom was still at the shop working, and he wanted something to eat. He came into my room where we were, asking why I didn't have his dinner cooked. Me being me, I responded with, "I'm not your wife; you been out all this time and didn't eat? You're not hungry then." He walked out of the room, cursing and going off. Within a few seconds, he came back into the room and jumped on me. While hitting me, he put his hands around my neck and began choking me. I began kicking and punching him, trying to get him off me. The kids were in an uproar, crying. At that moment, I punched him as hard as I could in the face, and he jumped up and walked out of the room. He went down the hall, into the den, and fell asleep on the couch. Within a few minutes, a car pulled up, and I heard the car horn beep three times. It was my cousin's daddy coming to pick her up. She grabbed her belongings and ran out the door to him as fast as she could.

I was still comforting my nephew, telling him everything would be okay while tears streamed down his face. My mom walked into the house and went into her room. I followed her and sat on the edge of her bed. I told her what had happened, and she responded with, "Are you serious," and just sat there. At first, I sat there in disbelief that he had just jumped on me. Then, got up, went into my room, and closed the door. Midnight approached, and I heard someone outside the house screaming, "Don't touch my sister again, or you know what's going to happen!" I jumped up and immediately started praying, tears streaming down my face while asking God, why me? My mom told my brother to go home and not get into trouble. Without much sleep at this point, I could see the sun begin to shine through my bedroom window. I got up and began packing my things up to head back to Birmingham after church. As I pulled up at church, contemplating going in, I waited a few minutes before getting out of the car. It was the first Sunday of the month. I was dreading after communion because all the deacons and pastors would line up while everyone shook their hands before leaving the church. As I got closer to my daddy, my heart started racing. As I approached him, I put my hand out, shook his hand without looking at him, and walked out the door. I left and got directly on the road without saying goodbye to anyone. Still traumatized about what happened at our house, I made a vow to myself that after I finished school, I would not be returning home.

Years went by, and I kept my promise to myself and started genuinely trying to figure this thing called life out. Not really having anyone to guide me, I made mistakes, fell, got back up again, and tried some more. I didn't know whom I could trust, so I kept everything inside. The older I grew, the more I began to resent my father; lowkey, I couldn't stand him. But then, therapy happened for me and changed how I viewed things in my life. As I reflected on how my dad grew up and his environment, I understood he was only a mirror of what he saw growing up. Now, I can see the changes he's trying to make, and I know that it won't happen overnight. Everything is worth a try, right?

Do I believe my daddy loves me? Yes! He tells me every time he talks to me. As you get older, it's harder to let go of the memories you never imagined that could've played a vital role in your life. You either let it continue to destroy you, or you pick up the pieces and build something beautiful out of it. See, my daddy made me strong, not because I wanted to, but because I didn't want anyone to have the opportunity to disappoint me. Hard work is what I know because I know I will not let myself down.

CHAPTER 3

Why Me

Death is something, as people, we don't like to think about but know we all must face one day. It was on August 8, 2008, the telephone rang early that morning, and the next thing I knew, I heard a scream get louder and louder. Soon after, my mom came into the room and told my brother and me to get dressed. My daddy rocked side to side with his head bowed as we headed out the door to the car, crying. Trin-i-tee 5:7's "Highway" was playing in the car, and at that moment, we entered the Medical Center parking lot. Knots took over my stomach as I was preparing for the worst. As we got off the elevator to the seventh floor, we were surrounded by family.

My mom and dad walked toward my grandmother's room while I stayed back. Instantly, my dad was calling for me.

"Ma Ma, I need you" repeatedly, he yelled out. My aunt came and grabbed my hand and took me into the room; I sauntered over to the bed where my dad was standing and looked at my grandmother's body lying still. Moments later, the monitor went off. As I looked up to read the screen, she flatlined. Screams came from all over the place in that room. As my heart dropped, my dad wrapped his arms around me and hugged me as tight as he could. I eventually got loose from him and ran out of the room.

As I headed back to the waiting room, I stopped, placed my back against the wall, with my hand over my face, and cried. I cried because I was sad. I cried because I was confused. I cried because I was young and had to watch my grandma die right before my eyes. I didn't quite understand what was happening right before my eyes, except I knew the pain was deep. My cousins, aunts, uncle, and family members were yelling, screaming, and falling out all over the place. You know *we* can be a little extra sometimes. Doing the absolute most. After an hour or so, we left the hospital, heading home. The sun was coming up, and my head was pounding.

Luckily, we didn't *have* to go to school that day, but I did miss the fact that I didn't get to go to school that day to see my boyfriend or *little friend,* as my mom would say. He was a year younger than me, and all the girls wanted him. That darn Triple D. We were inseparable and thought we had that love & basketball type of relationship. Wore the same number and everything. He even started running track with me, knowing he was slow, but he did it just to be around me, and I was here for it. My 8th-grade year was coming to an end I was transitioning to high school.

When becoming a teenager, you're not supposed to be worried about being perfect, just living a carefree teenage lifestyle. That wasn't the case for me. When you're a preacher's kid, all eyes are on you always. You have people constantly telling you how you should act, look, and dress, and it can be difficult trying to be something you're not. When you have the two-parent household every kid dreams of, but in the public eye, everything seems like gold, and behind closed doors, all hell is breaking loose. I walked around for years with a mean mug on my face because I was unhappy. Unhappy that I had a dad who stayed in the house but never spent quality time with my brothers or me because up the road was more important, or at least that's what it seemed like. How can you verbally translate that when you don't know how to express yourself authentically?

Central High School, home of the Red Devils, is where you'd find me from 2005-2009. As an athlete, my freshman year walking those halls were lit, like every day, lit. We had some of the best athletes come through there. For the next four years, volleyball, basketball, and track were my life. The track was my first love; I had been running for Coach Fortune since I was little. He had practically been a coach since my parents were in school. It all started with me running during the summer track season; the rest was history. Anytime I needed to release, stepping on the track and running was therapeutic for me, which was crazy because I didn't particularly like going outdoors unless I was running.

Sports taught me the meaning of discipline, perseverance, and teamwork. See, I was small, but I had the heart of a giant. On the volleyball court, I played the positions of setter and outside hitter. Your girl had ups. Basketball was a challenge for me, though, because of my size; I weighed a good 110 pounds. Coach W and I remained at odds, but as she would say, when I stopped talking, that's when you would need to worry. But as I got older and matured on and off the court and track, I finally understood what the meaning of silence meant.

Have you ever had a dream come true the same way you dreamed about it? Kind of like, déjà vu'. It was my senior year of high school, November 26, 2008, and we were playing our rival school, just like we did every year after Thanksgiving. That year, it was at Russell County High School, and the gym was packed with people standing up everywhere. It was the first quarter, and the opposing team was taking the ball out. They threw the ball inbounds, and I tipped it, caught it, and came down onto my knee. The gym went silent as I screamed at the top of my lungs, with tears coming down my face. My knee instantly swelled up, and the trainer came and took me off the court.

That following Monday, I went to the doctor to have my X-rays done. The doctor came in immediately afterward and told me it didn't look like I would be finishing my senior year out playing sports; I had a torn Mencius and an ACL tear. I was devasted because my senior year was my year, and I was looking forward to track season, but one incident had taken all of that away. Through the hurt I had, I told my doctor I was going to play ball, and he responded by putting me in a brace. I tried to play three games because

I wouldn't let myself quit, and each time I would turn the wrong way, my knee was shifting out of place, and I was being escorted off the court. At this point, I had no choice but to call it quits. It hurt so bad to see someone else wearing my number, but as a captain and a leader, I cheered them on every game.

January 11, 2009, was the day I was scheduled to have surgery for my recent injuries at Jack Houston Memorial Hospital. I didn't know what to expect, but after I got changed, they rolled me to the back to be examined from the waiting area. As I looked up, all I saw were bright lights, and the room temperature made me feel as though I was in Antarctica. All I could remember last was them asking if I was too cold, and then I woke up in the recovery room where my mom and brother were waiting on me. One thing about my brother was that he didn't miss a beat when it came to me, no matter what he had going on. As I lay there, the nurse came into the room and told me the doctor wouldn't discharge me until I threw up. Before she could finish talking and telling me that information, my head was in the trash can, and I was throwing up. My brother rolled me out of the door as my mom went and brought the car around.

On the ride home, I looked out the window and thought about what was next for me, but I had no clue, and I felt like my life was over. All I could think about was my senior year was now gone. After the injury, I was out of school for a couple of weeks, and while my parents went to work each day, my mom dropped me off at the Daniels' house. The Daniels family sure loved themselves some me. From the time I was there visiting, either Big D brought me breakfast in the morning when he got off work, or Mrs. Daniel cooked for me. They literally catered to me. Most days, I spent time in my room in the dark, with no tv on, no lights, no nothing, just complete silence, and darkness. It seemed as though I was escalating into a state of mind filled with melancholy and sorrow. Until one day when my mom came in and told me I was not going to let depression win, and I was going to get up from my bed. She opened the curtains to let some light in and started praying for me.

Therapy was a slow process for me; I hated it. I hated going so much to the point I did very little to help myself make progress toward healing. You wouldn't know if I didn't tell you that my right leg still isn't straight or healed to this day. That all came from me not taking therapy seriously when I was learning how to bend and get the full range of motion back to my knee. After some time, things got a little better, and I decided that I wanted a job to help my spare time pass by. Luckily, I was familiar with a manager at Zaxby's who hired me. I had played basketball with her grandson and went to the Boys & Girls Club of America with him for afterschool care, and she hired me at Zaxby's.

Everything started out great when I began working at Zaxby's until one night when we were closing. I was behind the front counter counting my register, and others in the lobby were sweeping and mopping. As quiet as a ninja, some 6 ft 5 man walks into the store with a gun; he doesn't say a word. He knew what part of the store to go to for the money. At first, everyone continued to perform their duties until I started seeing them jump across the counter into the back area of the store. I tried to run towards the back where everyone was going, but he grabbed me by my shirt and held the gun to the middle of my forehead. I couldn't utter a word. All I could do was raise my hand. Frightened that I would never see my family again, I quoted "Amazing Grace, how sweet the sound" for what seemed like forever. He looked me in my eyes, and after he got everything he wanted from the safe, he let me go and ran back out the front door. I ran towards the back, and the clowns wouldn't even let me out.

I turned around and ran out the front door. Just running. I don't know to where, but I ran as fast as I could. Once my coworkers realized it was me running, they chased after me and brought me back to the store. The nerve of them! And to make the situation worse, they were a group of all men. I returned to the store with blue lights flashing everywhere, and I had to give a statement. But how could I? I was in complete shock. Unfortunately, I had to drive home terrified from Bradley Park, in Columbus, GA, to the south side of Phenix City, AL. The entire drive, I couldn't stop looking in my rearview mirror, which felt like someone was watching me. Once I made it home, my parents greeted me at the door, with my mom crying and thanking God and my daddy for fussing and telling me I never have to work again in life. Which was a lie; I'm working now as I type this story.

CHAPTER 4

There is More

M iles College wasn't my first choice for higher education. Still, due to the circumstances and my late application, they were the first to reach out to me after I had already missed general admissions deadlines. The morning I was leaving for college, I heard a door slam in the front yard and someone yelling. I looked out my bedroom window to find my father crying and falling out into the grass. You would have thought someone had died or been seriously injured the way he was carrying on, but as I look back, those were happy tears that his baby girl was maturing and leaving home to obtain an education. As I approached the school, cars were everywhere, and I didn't know what to expect, but from the look of the building, I did know I didn't want to live in the freshman dorm. The only other dorm was Bass Hall for the upperclassmen and freshmen who were on Academic scholarships.

We cleaned and wiped everything as we unpacked the truck and loaded my things into the dorm room. Once we finished sanitizing, my roommate came in and introduced herself; I was puzzled. Not quite what I was expecting; I couldn't find a clean spot on her side of the room. There was trash everywhere I looked, not to mention the hair left all over the bathroom. I realized my roommate, this room, and the environment would be my life for the next four years. Within a couple of days, I adjusted a tad bit more until I walked into my dorm room one day. My roommate was eating all my delicious snacks... that she didn't ask my permission to eat. I automatically became aggressive with her and locked up all my belongings, including my television. I mean, she could've asked me first instead of welcoming herself to my property. To top the list off, she snored like a grizzly bear, and I was a light sleeper. So, I immediately started crying and called home because, for one, I wasn't used to sharing a room, and then to have someone breaking my sleep every night wasn't going to cut it for me.

My mom told me I could leave school and come home, but I told her I'd stay if she'd let me bring my car back to school. So, she agreed, and that following weekend I caught a ride home and drove my car back up the road. When I made it back to campus, I changed rooms from the 1st floor to the 2nd floor. At that moment, I knew the roommate lifestyle wouldn't be for me. Being observant and to yourself will really have people trying you. For example, every day, I would walk past Pitts Hall, and this big, tall girl would yell and roll her eyes when I walked by and say things like, "You must think you're better than somebody." Ironically, after some time, we got to know one another and became the best of friends.

Like most people starting college, I set a goal for myself to complete my undergrad program in four years. Most people doubted me and said I needed to only take twelve credit hours (4 classes) a semester because I was playing sports. They felt I wasn't able to handle a large workload. Being a biology major, you had a lab with every class, and though the hours were long, I wanted to prove my doubters wrong. My freshman year of college was exactly what I heard it would be. Partying throughout the week, watching the sororities and fraternities run the yard, cookouts, and more. Even with all that going on throughout the week, it never stopped me from attending Bible study on Wednesday nights and church on Sundays at Rock Church. At that time, going to church on Sunday mornings almost felt like going to a club like LR Hall on Saturday nights in downtown Birmingham.

I was still immature in my relationship with Christ, so Pastor Mike at Rock Church was very relatable and intriguing in his teachings; he made me want to learn more. I guess that scripture, "Train up a child in the way they should go and when they get older, they won't depart," is true. Throughout it all, God is the head of my life. In the past, I'd be bothered when I invited my friends to go with me, and their response was, "It doesn't take all that...I don't have to go to church to have a relationship with him, ... blah, blah blah." Nothing changed, but I kept God first in life. Since I was prohibited from not playing sports my first year, I still trained and worked as if everything I wanted was already mine.

It wasn't until one night, my friend Khadijah asked me to ride with her to see a high school friend of hers that I realized my relationship with God was getting stronger. Khadijah's friend lived off the Arkadelphia exit in

Birmingham. Khadijah was a giant, compared to me, and loud, but she was a gentle giant. I decided to go with her since I wasn't doing anything. We left out the door and headed towards Arkadelphia. We got off the exit and went to the Pilot gas station. As Khadijah exited the car, I told her I would stay inside, but she suggested I get out. Clueless, I looked around, trying to determine where her friend was. She tells me the person she would meet was "back there," and I'm like, "Back there, where?" At this point, I am nervous. We were at a truck stop in the dark, walking towards the back of the building, while male truck drivers were passing by, blowing at us and waving. Eventually, we made it to her friend's truck. Khadijah introduced us. They chopped it up for a minute, then we left. As we were leaving, the wind was blowing like crazy outside, and we decided to run back to the car. As we ran, we noticed a couple of men starting to chase us. Being a track star, of course, I left her in my dust. She yelled to me, "Cole, you're leaving me!" But I didn't care. I just wanted to get back to the car and back to safety. We made it back to the car, and Khadijah had forgotten that her driver's side door didn't work correctly. She threw me the keys to get into the car. I opened the door to let her in, and we sped off.

The men jumped into their car and started chasing us. But check this; we did not realize the men were undercover cops. We made it to the freeway and thought we could get away, not knowing a cop waiting for us at the bottom. All we saw were blue lights flashing, and I told her to pull over. She's yelling, " Cole, I can make it back to the campus!" I was like, "Not in this little Corolla!" So, she eventually pulled over. I asked her if she had any drugs while texting my brother, Dank. I told him that "if the Jefferson County Police Department called his phone, to please answer because we were about to get locked up." Khadijah told me to stop acting scared, and I told her I wasn't going to lie for her, and she'd be going to jail by herself. The next thing I knew, the cops were at both of our windows. They instructed us to get out of the car. I was so nervous; my body was shaking like a stripper. I exited the car and was told to sit on the curb. As I looked behind our car, I saw there were seven police cars lined up and were getting the K9 dogs out of the car.

I didn't know what was going on. I only knew that I was scared and my parents would get my tail. After about ten minutes, and many questions were asked by the cops, they finally decided to let us go and asked for our addresses.

We gave them the college's address, 5500 Myron Massey Blvd because we did not want them to send anything to our homes where our parents would be notified. The cops then told us that we should not go to any more truck stops because of the amount of prostitution that went on there, because prostitution was what they thought we were doing. Once we drove off from them, the car was as quiet as a mouse. As soon as we hit campus, I told her I'D never go anywhere else with her. If you know Khadijah, she gave an indifferent response, " I don't care, get out my car." I got out and slammed her door. She yelled at me, "Don't be slamming my door!" So, I yelled back with, "It's barely a door to slam," and went into my dorm. The entire situation had been more than crazy, but afterward, I began to realize that God was leading me to greater for my life; I just needed to get out of my own way for my triumph.

Days went by, and we'd ask each other if we had gotten any mail from the police yet. We would both laugh and say no. Summer was approaching, and I had convinced my mom to let me get an apartment off campus. She agreed but didn't want me to get a job because my studies were more important. The allowance she sent me every week, plus my monthly car payment and rent, was unmatched. I had it made compared to some of the other students and didn't realize how blessed I truly was at that moment. Life went on, we never heard anything else about that run-in with the police, and everything was good. Until one day, I saw a flyer while entering Taggert Hall on campus about an Alpha Kappa Alpha Sorority Incorporated interest meeting. I instantly took a picture on my phone, and excitement overcame me. I had always dreamed of being part of the AKA organization as a young child. I had experienced principals, teachers, coaches, church members, and women within the community who embodied every sense of the purpose of this illustrious Sorority. I loved how they served others and their community, not to mention they were some outstanding leaders.

I wasn't entirely sure how I would juggle everything. Classes were getting harder and required more study time. I was waking up at 4:30 am for practice. All this was taking a toll on me, but thanks to the support of my classmates, we all stuck together and made it happen. I called my Soror, Yolanda Daniel, and told her I wanted her to pin me as a new member of the sorority. She met me with excitement through the phone and wasted no time asking me who else would have done it. I laughed because I knew no one else could've taken her place. On November 11, 2012, I became a member of the first and finest sorority, Alpha Kappa Alpha Sorority Incorporated. Along with my thirty-eight beautiful line sisters, this is a bond I'll forever hold dear to my heart. Just like siblings, we fuss, laugh, and cry, but most importantly, we support and love each other. Things were going great for me, and I was later inducted into the Beta Kappa Chi Scientific Honor Society.

Track season came around, and my family came from out of town to watch me run at Birmingham Southern's campus. It was so good to see them in the stands. I stood in lane three, preparing for the 200-meter dash. I heard, "Runners take your mark." Walking toward the line to get in my block, I had my head down, with my hand in the correct position. As I set, the man raised the gun. After he fired it, I took off, hugging that curve as I led the race. Coming off the bend into the straightway, something shot up the back of my right leg, and I instantly grabbed my hamstring, going down. With tears streaming down my face and my leg in pain, my coach ran onto the track, picked me up, and carried me off. He said, "Damn, Toombs, that was your race," as he took me to the side of the track, to the trainers. It seemed as if I took a few steps forward, I'd just get knocked back down. It was the last meet of the season before the championship at Emory University. I was injured but determined to run. During my injury, I performed therapy twice a day and conditioned. Coach told me that I had to prepare for the *800*, which wasn't my race, but you run all distances when you're a runner.

Colleges from everywhere were present at the track meet. I checked in and warmed up for my upcoming race. There were three heats in the that particular race, and I was in the last one. Anticipation raised within me as I headed to the track. I stepped on with one goal in mind to make it to the finals. The gun went off, and I paced myself, staying with the pack for the first lap. With 300 meters left, my leg began bothering me, but I fought to the end and came in 4th. The championship came, and I was the only person left to compete in the finals from my school. However, I could not compete because my leg was swollen, and I was walking with a limp. All the way home, I looked out the window and questioned God why every time I got so close to winning, something occurred in my life and stopped what seemed like a victory. Have you ever felt that? Well, I've felt that way a lot throughout life. That was my last year running because I only had ten credits left to complete my degree and needed twelve total to be eligible to play sports for the following year. My Research and Biochemistry classes were the last two I needed to take before receiving my bachelor's degree in biology. Everything was going well in my life, and I had received my official graduation package, but I was still waiting for one professor to post my grade in Biochemistry. My classmates and I were on a ledge, waiting for that grade to be published. Once it came in, the entire class had failed. We were literally seven days away from graduation and were in an uproar because we wouldn't receive our degrees.

We went to the Dean and professors to see what we could do to resolve the issue with our grades. We even went to the chapel on campus to pray that God came through for us. The Dean went back and reviewed our previous assignments and grades and let us retake the final two days before graduation. We were told we had passed the class and could walk across the stage to graduate. What a miracle! May 21, 2013, I walked across the stage at graduation and received my bachelor's degree in biology. I felt joy because I had set a goal and accomplished it. However, that wasn't the end of my story that summer. I stayed with my brother, Damion, not knowing what was next at first. I was depressed because I would apply for jobs but would only be told that I was either overqualified or didn't have enough experience. How can you get experience if no one gives you a chance? After weeks of applying and getting turned down, I talked with my girl JC and decided to go to Nursing School.

Beginning that August, I was a student at the University of Alabama, preparing to enter my graduate program. Everything was so different. Going from a small HBCU school, where everybody was family, to a large PWI school, where you felt like an outcast, was a massive transformation. Attempting to learn the transit schedule, classrooms being filled with over 300 plus students, and having to make an appointment with your professor was a lot to grasp, but I was managing. After getting settled in, I had a meeting with my advisor. They informed me that I only needed to complete four classes to apply for the Nursing program since Miles didn't offer those classes. My brother Charles, a Stillman College student, visited to show me around Tuscaloosa and later told me he had a friend who was interested in me. I asked what he looked like, giving him a side-eye at the same time. He showed me a picture of Los, a football player, nicely built, with two gold teeth in his mouth. But a clean-cut guy overall.

Days went on, and Los and I became inseparable. We

did everything together, from studying, working out, cooking, and church. My neighbors were from Birmingham and went to Stillman, so Los introduced us, and they just so happened to be my sorority sisters. Except for one, Vi, she was a Delta. We became close and began hanging out all of the time. One day, my cousin Bee was headed out of town to her best friend's bachelorette weekend in Atlanta. After sending me pictures of her options, we finally agreed upon an outfit. At the end of our conversation, I told her to let me know when she made it back home. That night, I tossed and turned before eventually dosing off. The next morning came. As I was sound asleep, my cousin Stephanie called. I answered her call, and she told me that Bee was gone; I asked her what she meant by, 'gone.' She then screamed that Bee had been killed. I asked her who had done it, with my voice trembling. Stephanie told me it had been a car accident. I then checked my phone and noticed Bee had never texted me to let me know that she had made it home that night. The phone dropped from my hand as I screamed her name while tears streamed down my face. I picked up the phone to call my mom. No answer. I called my dad next, and he answered," Ma, what's wrong with you?" I mumbled, "Bee was killed in a car accident."

My dad hung up in my face, so I called Los and told him he had to come to take me to Birmingham. Bee was my cousin three years older than me; we were close. I couldn't believe she had left me like that. I was devasted, and the worst part was that I never got to say goodbye to her or see her one last time because she had a closed casket with no viewing. How could the one person who understood me be gone? I often questioned myself. Days passed, and I tried to cope with everything that had happened while completing my finals. Finals were over, and I made my way to the Nursing building to meet with my advisor. As I approached her door, a lady stopped me and asked if I was lost, and I told her I was looking for my advisor. She told me my advisor no longer worked for the university and asked how she could assist me. We went into her office, where she pulled up my information. The first thing out of her mouth was that I already had a degree from Miles College. Before I knew it, I responded with, "What that supposed to mean?" She said she hated to tell me that the curriculum had changed, and if I wanted to be a part of their Nursing program, I would have to start over by taking the University of Alabama classes. I told her I had initially been told they would accept my credits from Miles and that I wouldn't have attended their school if I knew I could not transfer my credits. She then told me that a school like Shelton State Community College or Jefferson State Community College would accept academic credits from Miles College, but not them.

After going back and forth with her, and her not wanting to direct me to someone else to speak with, I left the building, crying. I called my mom and told her what was going on. She told me to go back inside and not to leave the office until I got some answers. As I walked back in, office doors were closed in my face, and no resolution. Feeling like a failure, I went home and started packing my belongings, waiting on my apartment lease to end. I didn't quite understand the situation. My grades met their requirements, and I had done everything I was supposed to have done, to still end up rejected.

Lost and not knowing what was next for me, I landed back in Birmingham. Los visited me since he had just graduated from Stillman and told me he would begin working out of state soon. When I told my mom my decision, she was upset and didn't mind voicing her opinion. She told me straight out, "God not gone bless no mess while you trying to shack up." Yes, I was taught not to shack up until you're married all my life. Frustrated, I told her she had done it and had two kids before marriage. What was the difference? She replied, "When you know better, you do better." After everything I had just gone through, I wasn't trying to hear that. She stopped sending me money, stopped paying my phone bill, and told me I could take care of myself since I thought I was grown. I immediately panicked, "How the heck I'm about to make it with no job?" The next day rolled around, and I went to Miles to help a student. While there, I ran into Football Coach Ruffin. He told me they needed a Head Coach for the Track team and asked me if I wanted to take the job. Without hesitation, I said yes, and a sigh of relief left.

Not knowing what I was going up against, I took the job at Miles and performed it based on everything I was once taught. Boy, that position matured me quickly. Coaching adults near your age while being challenged daily, and let's not talk about the unprofessionalism coming from my colleagues. The environment was a lot to handle, but I loved track and field. I loved how I connected with different types of women and instilled some wisdom and knowledge into each of them. While coaching, I had two team members achieve a ranking at the State-wide Competition, but that still wasn't enough for me. I wanted more but didn't know exactly what that more was. After a year and a half, I left coaching and started working for the Federal Government. Everything was smooth sailing. I got pushed out of my comfort zone by leading meetings, mentoring, and working on projects. It helped bring me back out of my shell.

There was a time when speaking in front of a crowd used to be something that came very naturally. One day, an elderly church lady told me that I talked too much and needed to stop trying to be the center of attention all the time. Her comment really did something to me. It placed me in a shell, and the confidence I once had was gone. I went from an outspoken little girl to a young woman who didn't know how to use her voice. Each time I was asked to do something, I declined because I didn't want to be the center of attention. Her words followed me for years. The more I was pushed to lead I began gaining my confidence back. One day, a lady approached me to train her because she wanted to live a healthier lifestyle. In my mind, I didn't think I was qualified enough for that, and she needed to get someone else to do it. She was adamant that she needed my help. I went home that night, prayed about it, and asked God if training her was what I needed to do. From that moment, I received my certification to become a personal trainer.

My focus wasn't just on the physical body but on the mind and spirit also. All it took was my first client, and women from everywhere began reaching out to me. In the training group, we encouraged one another. Some got to know who God was, learned how to pray, and how to become a better version of themselves.

CHAPTER 5

Betrayal

Betrayal often doesn't come from someone you don't know. It's always the ones closest to you. It doesn't matter how good or respectful you are. They'll find anything to envy you about.

Sophomore year in high school, I met this young lady, JC, during a volleyball tournament, and we became close friends. She was from across the water and went to Northside High School, while I attended Central High, home of the Red Devils. Neither of our teams didn't really see competition until we hit the floor to battle each other. There was one game where the ball was set to me, and I went up to spike the ball, and it hit her dead in the face. Words were exchanged as she went into a rage and vowed I had done it on purpose.

Eventually, she got over it, and we became close friends. We hung out and supported each other when the other needed it. We were complete opposites; she was loud, funny, and a bit of a mystery because you never knew what she would have up her sleeve. After high school, she attended Troy University, and I went to Miles College. After I graduated in 2013, I didn't know what was next for me in life, but I did know I wanted to go to Nursing School. Though I wanted more education, I became frustrated because I didn't want to be in debt by going back to school. Still, I knew I just wanted to be successful, so I did what I had to do. In the summer of 2013, I was at my brother's home and on the phone with JC, discussing our next moves.

Fall rolled around, and we both were attending the University of Alabama, in Tuscaloosa, together for graduate school. Fall rolled around, and it was time to start a new chapter in our lives. JC loved to cook, so Sunday, after we settled into our apartments in the Woodlands Apartments, she decided we'd cook a Sunday dinner. My brother, Charles, who was attending Stillman then, came over and asked if he could bring his homeboy with him. I told him it was totally fine. They arrived that evening, and we all were just chopping it up and chilling. That following night, my brother came and told me his friend wanted to get to know me and asked if it were okay if he gave him my number. I told him sure. The next day came, and my brother's friend asked if he could come to see me after his practice. He did, and we hung out. The rest was history from there.

JC came home one afternoon and decided she wanted to have a talk with me. I was clueless about what she wanted to talk about because she always had an issue or problem going on. She told me I didn't need to be hanging around my homeboy, Los, a lot because there were plenty of more dudes here to choose from. She suggested that I may like those men more. I stopped her in her tracks and informed her that school was my priority and he was just a friend. Puzzled and with a confused face, I asked her if there was a problem or did she just not want him around. She responded with, "Well, you know I don't like to walk around in clothes all the time, and I don't think I would be comfortable if he saw me," she says. After hearing her explanation, I called bullshit from a mile away. If you know, then you know. As time passed and he came around her, she would have a nasty attitude and make smart remarks.

This was all good and well until one day; I walked to my neighbor's apartment to study for a big test we had coming up. I left my door unlocked because Los was upstairs, and I wouldn't be gone but for an hour at the least. I arrived back home and noticed the door was locked. I began banging on my apartment door, calling his phone, banging again, and calling his phone. I soon heard somebody inside, running down the stairs inside our townhouse. It was him. As I walked into the house, my so-called friend was in the kitchen with her panties and bra on. I immediately went off, yelling and screaming at her. She responded by stating this was *her* apartment, and she was free to wear what she pleased. One part of me wanted to fight, and the other part realized she didn't know any better. From that day forward, we barely spoke, and she stayed away from the apartment most of the time.

Life went on, and I moved back to Birmingham, Al. Everything was going fine, and Los barely would be home because he worked in North Dakota. Seven days out of the month, he'd be home. As time progressed, things weren't quite the same between him and me anymore. Eventually, I knew I had to leave the relationship. Have you ever had that feeling or urge about things no longer serving your purpose? Well, that's how I felt; things were different. When he came home from work one night, I told him I was leaving the relationship, which led to an argument, and he left the apartment. Since our lease wasn't up until January, it was July when I told him I was leaving.

Every night up until it was time to move out, he would come in the house late, bearing gifts and being loud. While all this was happening in that relationship, JC asked me if I wanted to go on a trip with her. However, I noticed she was in Birmingham every day from her postings on social media, but I was confused because she had told me she was in Augusta, Georgia. I kept seeing pictures of her with a male on social media every day, but his face was never shown. If you're anything like me, you pay attention to details. Like, a person's clothing, all the way down to their walk. I told my brother, Charles, I knew it was Los I had seen in the photos. Charles was in denial at first. Well, moving day came, and I was ready to move out and start my new chapter. That day, Los left the house, fully dressed for work, at 7 am, when he didn't have to be there until 12 pm. The movers came, and I moved all my things and began to get settled into my new place. Being excited about this new beginning quickly became a feeling of disappointment the following weekend.

It was the morning of Saturday, October 2nd. I was sitting in my living room watching television when my phone started going off hysterically. As I picked up the phone to see who it was, I noticed I had ten text messages from JC. Upon opening the messages, I could see they were pictures and videos of her in my home, with him, in my bed, and much more. Instantly, I called his phone, and he had blocked me. She and I were going back and forth through texts. All I could see was red. My chest was hurting (REAL BAD). I posted a picture she had sent me of them together on my Snapchat. People were telling me I needed to delete it and choose a higher route to go down in this situation; they insisted I be the bigger person. But how can you choose the higher road when your close friend has been in your house, without your knowledge, in your bed, and is now dating your ex-boyfriend? No telling how long their little fling had been going on. I sat on my living room floor and cried because I couldn't understand the betrayal that just had happened. My emotions would only allow me to feel like, why me?

Shortly after, to save face, she told the world that she didn't know who I was and that we were never friends. Then she turned around and lied on my God, saying He put them together!

One of my "big sisters" came and picked me up shortly afterward, and we went riding, looking for them. The first stop we made was his job at AT&T on Lakeshore Parkway in Birmingham. His former coworker told me he no longer worked there, and they didn't know his whereabouts. So, we left and went to Homewood because the word was that she lived in some apartments over there. We rode down each row of apartment buildings, searching for her car, only to end up empty-handed. Looking at my phone, I wondered how, even when this could happen when she couldn't even stand him. Or was that all a front?

Weeks and months went by, and there was still no sign of them like they had just disappeared. Until one night, my friend Tay was slaying my hair, and the girlfriend of one of his homeboys invited me to her boyfriend's party. I hesitated at first, but then I said, "Might as well." I showered, put on this super cute dress, then headed out the door downtown. As I walked through the door of the party, I saw him sitting down in front of a sitting booth. I spoke and kept it moving. Some time had passed, and I wasn't even interested in what he had going on or him and JC. That's when things started to get weird for me. One couple near me decided they wanted to go outside and take a smoke break when smoking was allowed in the club. So, I sat there, watching things unfold. A guy came up to me and told me to stay right here.

Confused about what was going on, I stayed right there, sipping on my drink. I then looked up, and JC was walking through the door with her friend. I instantly thought I was being set up because why would you invite me to a place knowing the situation and our history? It didn't take long for those emotions to come back to me. As I sat there with a table between Los and me, she stood in front of him with his back towards me, saying, "Bae, I'm about to beat this B*tch ass "repeatedly. She had one more time to say that before I hopped up from my seat and flew around to the other side of the table. Los greeted me halfway, trying to stop me, and before I knew it, he was catching blows from my fist, left and right. All the while, he's asking why I was doing this. It wasn't about him, but my respect and I was going to make him feel me on that. My homeboy Gee then came and grabbed me. He told me to go home because none of my actions that night were in my character, and I was entirely out of character. He walked me out of the club and to my car. He didn't leave until I pulled off. My brother's number was on speed dial. So, I called him, yelling and going off. He told me to go home because if I continued, I would end up sitting in the Jefferson County jail for the weekend and that we'd deal with JC and Los later.

Later never came, but *KARMA* did, and it hit harder than I could've imagined...

CHAPTER 6

Harassment

December 8, 2020, I closed on my newly-constructed home in Alabama. Like most realtors, they posted the closing via social media with me holding the sold sign. I had many people congratulating me and wishing me the best. Until I looked in my Messenger app on Facebook and saw where this man had written me a message, saying, "Congratulations, let me know when the housewarming is." I responded with, "Thanks, LOL, I got you." He replied, "I'm for real now." Then after the encounter, I began wondering how we had become Facebook friends. Just like most Facebook users, I didn't know who half of the people I interacted with were.

I had only seen this man at church, and before that, we had never had a conversation or anything. From that day forward, he continued to write me messages on Messenger. When I logged onto Messenger, sometimes, I would respond. Until one day, he asked for my phone number since I would take longer than he liked for me to write him back. He then sent me a message detailing a run-down of his life. After that message, I still hesitated and waited a while before I just gave him my number. He would call me sometimes, I would answer sometimes, and some I didn't. So, then he wanted me to download the Duo application because he didn't have an iPhone to Facetime. All of this was so weird to me that one day I told my therapist about it, and she told me something seemed off and to just be careful.

Towards the end of December, there were Christmas tournaments held at Hoover High School for basketball. I had gone with my friend because her husband coached for another school. The man who had sent the Messenger messages came over and spoke to me, and we chopped it up. He proceeded to ask what I was doing afterward, and we met at Surin West and ate. Time went on, and we would gradually talk, but it never developed into anything serious. Until one day, he had the nerve to tell me I had too many homeboys and that I needed to get rid of them. I thought, "Umm, sir, my friends were here before you, and they'll be here after you're gone," I responded. He decided to get aggressive and repeat himself, thinking that would change what I had said.

As the discussion escalated, he tried to put the "WORD OF GOD "on me and told me that "if I wanted a husband, I needed to learn to be submissive and listen and stop being a smart ass all the time." He would ask me if I had read and reflected on my daily devotional. If I told him that I had focused on a different one, he would tell me that God would punish me because I was supposed to be following him. Obviously, he didn't know the type of woman he was talking to. So, I started distancing myself from him and let him know that I had my own relationship with Christ. He had a mobile detailing service, and I wanted to support it. So he came out and washed my car one day at my home. After he left, I assumed he thought about it on his visit because he asked me how many rooms I had. Can you believe he had the audacity to ask me if he and his kids could move in?

He started telling me that I was everything he wanted in a wife. He added that he needed a wife so that his youngest daughter could have a mother because his ex-wife was deceased. And, for me, that was probably the next red flag.

Ultimately, I had to have this talk with my therapist because there was no way he was talking to me like that. She told me he was controlling and some other things, and I needed to slowly start pulling myself away. So, I took her advice. I limited the number of times I would answer, so I really wasn't answering his calls anymore, and he would literally blow me up and text until I did. After that, I told him I couldn't be friends with him anymore because he was doing too much, and I was not here for all the extra stuff that he'd been bringing into my life. Of course, he wanted to play the victim and hit me with a sad story about people leaving him and not having anyone there to be a friend or listening ear. But I wasn't buying it, and the answering became less and less. And my rage became more and more intense, with yelling.

I didn't know how to just make him leave me alone altogether because simply voicing that to him wasn't working. So, a friend of mine suggested I post a picture on my Instagram story of myself and another man holding hands at the table, which should make him get the picture. Whew! He went the f^*k off on me verbally, and it was horrible. At that point, I had already blocked his number from my phone. So, he sent me an essay-length message on Instagram, and I ignored him. It was three o'clock in the morning, storming outside, and my phone went off. He had sent me a message going off on me and saying a bunch of wild, crazy things toward me.

The moment I received his message, I was wide awake and couldn't go back to sleep. Scared, I proceeded to call my homegirl, who came from Calera, to my house to stay with me that night. By the time she had arrived, the sheriff was pulling up to my home. They walked around the house to ensure everything was safe and secure and advised they'd be patrolling the area for the next couple of days. Regardless, I couldn't sleep. I called my big brother, who lived in Atlanta because I needed to just tell someone of all the craziness I had been enduring, and I didn't want my parents to worry. The sun finally came out, and I called my guy friend to come over. He was so puzzled by my story because he couldn't believe everything I told him.

He then wrapped his arms around me and told me he had me, would take good care of me, and protect me. I didn't want to bring this drama into his life, so I told him he didn't have to communicate with me anymore. He told me he wasn't going anywhere, reached in his pockets, pulled out a gun, and told me to always keep this on me for protection. Due to the fact I was once held at gunpoint, I began to have an anxiety attack because I was having flashbacks, but I kept it under control because he didn't know at the time. He headed towards the door and assured me he was one call away. I felt a wave of peace come over me.

After all that action with *Mr. Messenger Man*, I had to call into work that day because I was restless and needed some sleep. That didn't stop my afternoon gym training, though. But I couldn't fake it in front of my clients; they knew something was off, but I had to show up for them. I was afraid to go home because *Mr. Messenger Man* was still messaging me from both Facebook and Instagram nonstop, commenting on things I'd posted. He'd get even angrier with me if I deleted his comments. What do you do when you don't know what to do? I called a friend of mine that was a sheriff. I told him the situation so he could put out a restraining order; however, he told me that the next time the guy reached out, I needed to tell him to stop. Then I'd be able to move forward with the restraining order. Unfortunately, he didn't message me or call. This guy had followed my friends and sent them all messages trying to persuade them to get me to respond to him.

He even reached out to the lady who styled and

maintained my dreadlocks and asked when I was coming to get my hair done because he knew my birthday was coming up. My friends called me, ranting about him and worried because they knew nothing of how the situation escalated between him and me. One morning, a client and I were walking into the gym. I noticed his car was parked outside, and as we walked by it; my heart was beating what felt like 100 beats per second. And as I walked in the door, I asked the guys at the front desk If they knew if the person in the red truck parked outside was actually inside the gym. They said no one had ever gotten out of the car. At that next moment, we saw the car pulling out of the parking lot. I had to pull myself and my emotions together quickly because I still had to work that evening, training my clients. So, I cut on my Gospel music and prayed to myself.

I took another day off from work because, at this point, I was stressed to the extent I couldn't eat, and my weight was drastically declining. I went from 145 pounds to 123 pounds in a matter of months. I was embarrassed about what I was going through in my personal life. Not to mention people making statements to me that I shouldn't lose any more weight and having them continuously asking me if I was okay. I slept in the daytime and was up all night, waiting with the gun in my hand. Once I had gotten to this point, he was officially blocked from my social media accounts and cell phone. I was just starting to feel a little more comfortable until I started receiving calls from an app where he used a fake phone number. One night, leaving Urban Smoke restaurant, he messaged me again from the app and told me to have a talk with him. I told him I was not going to talk with him and he needed to leave me alone.

He told me he was going to be parked outside my house and not to be afraid. I told him the police would be waiting on him if he did. As I got closer to my exit, he blew up again with fury at me. I didn't want to go home because I was so alarmed and petrified. I kept driving beyond my house and called my best friend, Gee, but he told me he couldn't help me right then because he was in Montgomery. My mind was so panicked and clouded that I couldn't think of anyone else to call. So, I ended up driving to the Embassy Hotel in Hoover to get a room for the night. Then, I thought about my friend, Tika, that lived close to me and told her the situation and asked if I could stay the night at her house.

It was nobody but God. She responded and told me to come on over. As I arrived at her house, my phone was still going off with notifications from him asking if I would just have a conversation with him. I accepted his offer, hoping he would leave me alone afterward. Forever. As he was going on and on, he missed his exit from the interstate and quickly realized he was in West Blockton. In an uproar, he started having a panic attack because he did not know how to find his way out. I hung up the phone on him. I messaged his friend and told him to reach out to his friend because he just wouldn't stop attacking me. As I awoke the following day, I had a missed call with a voicemail from his mother. Yeah, you heard me right, his mother, telling me that I needed to call her, that this entire situation was a trick of the enemy, and that she wanted to pray for me.

My exact thought was, "wtf was next? will this be never-ending?" Did I mention he was a minister at my church? When the therapy session rolled around, my therapist told me I needed to reach out to the Pastor of the church and let him know what was going on since I was on their Prayer Team. Members of the Team had been reaching out to me because I had stopped serving and wouldn't respond to any of them. I thought to myself, "Where was God? How could he be letting me go through this?" These types of thoughts consumed my head on a daily basis. As I walked into Target one evening, on 150 in Birmingham, my phone rang. It was a minister who was also my sorority sister. She told me she had been worried about me because I hadn't been serving at church.

I initially hesitated to tell her what was going on because the fact of the matter was that then, I didn't know whom I could trust. My guard was entirely up with everyone I came into contact with. I reluctantly gave her a brief synopsis of what I was dealing with in the situation, and she stopped me in my tracks and informed me that she knew all about the circumstances surrounding what I was talking about. She knew because *Mr. Messenger Man* had reached out to a few ministers and Prayer Team members. He'd confessed to them that God told him that a distinct young woman in the church was his wife, we were going through some things, and the young woman was someone on the Prayer Team. Now, at this point, I'm confused because these people absolutely believed him. I told the minister that *Mr. Messenger Man's* entire confession was a lie and that we had never been mutually exclusive, and right now, I needed some time away from the congregation and physical church. From that moment, I never wanted to step foot in a church again.

My brother's homeboy contacted *Mr. Messenger Man* to tell him to chill out with his interactions with me because he was going too far. But guess what. *Mr. Messenger Man* manipulated my brother's friend so well that he had the nerve to be on the phone praying for him. At this point, I was just ready to give up because, as you see in today's world, nobody believes you until it's too late. *Mr. Messenger Man* then started sending videos crying, saying God told him to hold on to me, but I told him to let me go. He started appearing at every home game Miles College had, watching me, and asking people close to me where I was going at night so he could show up. My brother's line brother was starting to get upset because this guy relentlessly questioned him about me. He finally confessed, "Cole, if this man says one more thing about you, he gone meet his maker."

When will enough be enough? Nobody believes you until something happens!

Depression, fear, anxiety, and doubt all made me feel defeated. I didn't want to be on Earth anymore. The thought of leaving this world consumed my mind daily. My close circle of friends was my strength from the moment I told them what was going on in my personal life until I gained enough strength to fight the battle. I prayed and cried and prayed and cried because I believed in God. Still, I didn't understand how a person who stood before his people in the church and proclaimed the Gospel could be so freaking sick-minded. My faith was gone. Every day we see how these abusive situations play out in this world and the men who can't handle rejection prey on their victims. You never know how these situations could affect you until you stand in those shoes. As time passed by, the number of fake phone numbers he was calling from began declining and eventually stopped.

I never thought I would be a victim of stalking and harassment, but thank God, he kept me covered under his wings.

Psalms 91:4 He shall cover thee from the snare of the fowler, and from the noisome pestilence.

CHAPTER 7

Forgiveness

Forgiveness is the action or process of forgiving or being forgiven. Often when someone hurts us, whether intentionally or by mistake, we have two options. We can either forgive them or hold on to whatever they did. Is forgiving someone helpful to our lives? Can we benefit from it? In Matthew 6:14-25, the Bible says that if you forgive others when they sin against you, your Heavenly Father will also forgive you. But if you do not forgive others of their sins, your Father will not forgive your sins. Is it worth holding on to what someone has done to you?

Learning how to forgive did not happen overnight for me. Growing up, you hear, forgive and forget. How can you forgive someone and forget what they've done? And forgive someone who has caused you pain when the memories still haunt you? That offense will always be in the back of your head, reminding you of what happened. I was always taught to forgive, but it wasn't until I was in my late twenties that I understood the concept of forgiveness and letting go. Forgiveness does not mean revenge. There is something powerful in forgiveness; when you choose to release it, you can change your life and the people you encounter. God used everything that happened to me, made me better, made me stronger, gave me wisdom, gave me insight, and taught me about myself.

What stops us from forgiving others? Most times is because we only see the pain from our perspectives. Is it our larger-than-self egos or pride making us think we can 'get our lick back'? Everything that happened to you was for a lesson, and it was ordained to get something out of you. But, you must see the lesson connected to the situation and what the lesson is trying to teach you. It may teach you that every wound leaves a scar, and every scar tells a story. You don't have to live the rest of your life in regret for what you didn't do because your pain stopped you. The Bible tells us in Peter 5:10 that the good thing about all that is after you have suffered a while, He will establish you and make you perfect. Not meaning what happened to you didn't matter, but meaning it was for a purpose to be fulfilled through you.

Forgiveness requires faith, and faith begins where understanding ends. Faith is not found in what you believe in but in **whom** you believe in. It will be unfamiliar and force vulnerability and the constant state of being uncomfortable. God knows the situation better than you; he has a plan for whatever caused you pain. But it takes faith to believe that, and on the other side, know God is with you. Know that in your valley, while you are down, God is teaching you what the mountaintop could have never taught.

My parents were not always available to be present at all my games. It taught me that when I have kids, I must make time and be present for them. Had I not become injured, I would not have been taught how much care and stretching are needed for my body. Had I not been betrayed by my friend, I would not have been taught that everybody who calls themselves your friend isn't your friend and that some people only want what you have. Had I not been held at gunpoint, I would not have been taught I should not take life for granted because it can be taken away from you in the blink of an eye. Had I not been harassed, I would not have been taught that everyone isn't who they say they are and everybody doesn't deserve access to you, even if it's a member of your church.

Going through life, I always had one question in the back of my mind, "WHY ME?" What did I ever do to deserve to be treated that way? They say God gives his most challenging battles to his strongest soldiers, but in my defense, that wasn't me. Soft life, what is that? I never got the opportunity to be soft or open because no one ever created that space for me. I always had to keep my guard up so no one could think they could play with me. I thought I knew myself well, but it wasn't until I had pain that I discovered I only knew a little portion of myself. I went through life bottling everything inside until I met my friend, JT. JT would always correct me in love. I could talk to him about anything. He prayed for me daily, encouraged me, pushed me to be better, and constantly reminded me who I was. It was different because I wasn't used to it, but then I realized this was troubling me, and I needed some help with the issue. Google became my best friend as I searched for black women therapists in the Birmingham, Al, area. Eventually, I stumbled across a professional named Crystal Mullen-Johnson. Her accolades were outstanding, and her online reviews from other patients let me know she was the right one for me.

For so long, I had put everyone else's needs and wants before mine, and I realized it was time to put Nicole first. I kept entering repeated cycles that weren't getting me anywhere but back to the starting point. I wanted better and to be a better version of myself. I pleaded for change. It was time for me to heal from past traumas and hurt. Often, we only touch things at the surface because most people thrive on getting attention while being broken instead of getting healed. I knew I had to do better if I wanted better, and better started with me. Session one with my therapist came around, and she asked me why I was there and what I wanted to get from this. "Here we go again," I said to myself, looking at her in the video of my iPad since we were in a pandemic and sessions weren't being held in person.

One thing I was taught before I started healing was that if you want a positive outcome, you must be honest in everything. Healthy boundaries, assertive language, core beliefs, self-care, and habits, to name a few, helped me with each session I went through. At the end of year one in therapy, we completed an evaluation to see how much I had progressed. She was pleased with the outcome, but I knew some work still needed to be done. We went from two sessions a month to just one, and I couldn't have been prouder of myself for my progress. Until one day, we talked about loneliness, and something in me got triggered. I burst into tears during the session. We were in complete silence for about two minutes before I started apologizing for crying. My therapist reassured me it was safe to let it out.

At that moment, it was as if my mind went back to my childhood, and I was replaying events when my parents weren't there or when I wasn't protected. Anger took over, and I asked the question once again, "WHY ME?" Why were the streets so important to my father? Why did he have to jump on me? Why did my mother think she couldn't miss just one church event so that she could tend to her family? What felt to me like I was back at square one was nothing but healing taking place. I had to get to the root of the problem, the source of where it all started. Once I was able to get to the core and uproot that thing that had a hold on me, healing was able to take place. That wound turned into wisdom. I had to let go and forgive. Holding on did nothing for me but make me angry and hold onto resentment. You must keep your eyes open and face the tough times, even when afraid because there is another you that's waiting to be whole. Wholeness gives you a new lease on life. Wholeness will break generational curses and give you generational blessings. The curse ran through my family until it ran into me. Once I healed, the curse was broken.

Psalms 34:18-19 The Lord is close to the brokenhearted and saves those who are crushed in spirit. You may have many troubles, but the Lord will deliver you from them all.

CHAPTER 8

New Beginnings

As time goes by, you often wonder if growth even matters or if things can stay the way they are. As I look back, I realize if I wasn't ever faced with adversity, I wouldn't know how to overcome it. New Beginnings aren't always about starting fresh; a new beginning is learning from the different lessons you went through and how not to make that same mistake twice. Your scars either worked for you or against you. The suffering made a demand on what God placed inside of me, and I had to learn not to be imprisoned in my past. Just because it's the truth doesn't mean I had to navigate my life off the compass of what I saw. Truth is, I'm not qualified, but I dared to get up and go after it. The good is connected to the call, and if you say no to the call, you forfeit the blessing that's connected to your obedience. But first, I had to get out of my own way and let God be God. Most people love the thought of being chosen or great at something. Those whom God is going to use the most, he crushes the most severely. What happens when you're placed in the refining process and crushed?

It will be difficult at first, but you must be honest with yourself. Here is what most people don't realize success is directly impacted by your self-development. If you don't prioritize working on yourself and your self-growth, the likelihood of you reaching your goals will be slim. You must go through some things and some pain to be anointed. The only way you can receive the anointing is by being crushed. The Garden of Gethsemane on the Mount of Olives that's the place where olives are pressed for oil. In Matthew 26, Jesus went the night before he was crucified. The sin of the world had come upon him and pressed down like olives. Even if Jesus is the savior of the world, he still had to endure all the challenges we now face today. It's a cost you must pay. It's a process you must go through, and know that broken things are still beautiful. How much are you willing to endure to get to the other side?

Be courageous because it will not always be easy. Be bold; you must dare to step into those moments and become someone in your life whom you're willing to die for that old version of. The suffering isn't the end of you. The word states that the pain cannot compare to the joy that's coming. God turned everything that looked like turmoil around for me. The suffering taught me to have boundaries and to be humble in every area of my life. I'm glad I suffered so no one else must. God chose me for this very moment to let others know that he had already paid the price. We just have to follow his lead. In time everything will work out for your good.

I was broken, but now I'm healed. I was lost, but now I'm found. I was walking in shame, but God lifted my head and restored me. Even when I didn't have a father's touch, I had my heavenly father who protected me, loved me, and guided me every day of my life. To have a touch of your heavenly father is to know you'll always be safe in his arms. But first, you must get to know who your heavenly father is. I had to build a relationship with him, talk to him daily and read his words. Through it all, my hope was restored; I had faith again. I didn't have faith because things got better. I had faith because of whom I believed in. God never left my side. He was there, preparing me to live out the purpose he has for my life. I had to learn that there is strength in being vulnerable. The moment I stopped trying to be in control of my life, that's when things shifted for me. I knew God changed me where I once used to ask for things the world could give me. I started asking him for things the people couldn't give me peace, joy, wisdom, and knowledge. It's not that I live, but Christ lives in me. He took me on a path to discover him in ways no one could have taught me.

I can now say I'm free from all the things that once had me bound. Letting go wasn't easy, but it was necessary.

ACKNOWLEDGMENTS

God, thank you for always leading and guiding me, for I could not have done this without you.

To my mother, thank you for every prayer you've prayed and lesson you've taught me.

To my father, thank you for teaching me how to overcome.

To my grandmother, Rena, thank you for always believing in me.

To my brothers, thank you for always being my protectors and having my back, no matter what obstacles came my way.

To my girls, Stephanie, Takeita, and Kimberly, thank you for staying by my side and lending me a shoulder in my darkest moment.

To Dr. Ty, thank you for walking this path with me as I wrote this book.

To my therapist, thank you for the necessary tools you've given me to help on my healing journey.

To my friend, Pastor JT, thank you for encouraging me and being the light I needed in the midst of darkness.